FOREWORD

The original idea for this publication was conceived as long ago as 1994 and was then to be titled "M
work was never published. Instead, the video film, "A Sentimental Journey" took its place. The cor
and this was achieved with a classic motor car, travelling through the streets of Old Gainsborough.

Using original cine and stills the film achieved its original aim to show Gainsborough as it was.

The first half of the twentieth century saw little change in the layout and character of the town. The second half saw Gainsborough change beyond recognition.

Change. The word has many connotations. Some changes can be for the better – some for the worse. Judge for yourself.

Chris Keeling resurrected the original idea of Memories for You, in this publication. A non pretentious reflection of how a town, ravaged by war, began to hold its head up high again.

Gainsborough has a local history group called The Delvers and many of these original photographs were taken by them. Others were given or loaned by local people.

Some photographs featured are professional and many were originally available through picture post cards. The Delvers wish to express their gratitude to all the original photographers, too many to name individually, who have helped make this publication possible.

The journey you are about to take is possible today and in some small way it is the authors' hope that this will encourage participation in the Delvers local history tours of Gainsborough.

The Delvers are always interested to hear of personal memories connected to the places and names of Old Gainsborough. Please feel free to contact us if you have a special story to share.

From the comfort of your own armchair, now sit back and travel back in time. Enjoy the journey. Enjoy, All Our Yesterdays.

Darron Childs
darron.childs@btinternet.com

Index

Published by Arc Publishing and Print
166 Knowle Lane
Sheffield
S11 9SJ

Telephone 07809 172872

INTRODUCTION

I was born in Gainsborough and have lived in the town all my life. I have also seen the town change beyond recognition.

The Gainsborough I grew up in has gone - yet I remember it like yesterday.
Of Modern Gainsborough, I particularly like the Riverside Walkway and Whitton's Gardens.

It has also been pleasing to see the town's entertainment venues of my youth, such as the Town Hall and The State once again come back to life in recent years.

This bygone reflection will take you back in time, allowing you to once again enjoy, All Our Yesterdays.

Thelma Childs

This book is dedicated to Annie Howitt-Cowan

(1953) The people of Gainsborough were thankful that their town had survived the war. Their town had changed little over the last fifty years – but they probably could not imagine just how much it would change over the next fifty years! A Coronation Street Party in Hawksworth Street, and later tea at the Café Hylton, is being celebrated in this photograph.

Chapter One: The Old Hall   The home of The Hickman & Bacon families

(c. 1910) The Medieval Manor House known locally as The Old Hall. The Lord of the Manor moved to a new residence at nearby Thonock in around 1720. This photograph was obviously taken before the Cenotaph was added.

(c. 1920) Depicting the first Cenotaph, in the grounds of the Old Hall. It collapsed into one of the town's many tunnels, prompting another site to be found on the corner of the Old Hall grounds.

(c. 1990) A delightful winter view of the Old Hall showing the Oriel Window. Once a significant display of wealth and power, the Manor of Gainsborough was purchased by Sir William Hickman in 1596.

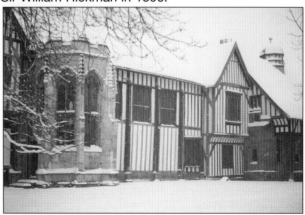

CASTLE HILL WALK, GAINSBOROUGH.

(c. 1950) Castle Hill Walk, later known as The Avenue, is the road that led to Thonock Hall, the last home of The Lord of the Manor. This countryside scene is today a busy road with a housing development.

(c. 1920) The Hunt at Thonock Hall. A now forgotten image, as the Hall was bulldozed during the 1960s. Today the site is the home of Ping Golf (Europe). The Hall is best remembered as the venue for the Co-op gala, with decorated drays, pulled by horses. The whole event was a fabulous day of fun geared towards entertaining the towns' children.

(c. 1920) The Riverside, before the new walkway. One of the old basket works to the left of the picture is visible near Dog Island.

(c. 1960) Barge passing the little cottages (now demolished) which backed up to the river from Bridge Street.

(c. 1990) Mills and warehouses facing the River Trent. In recent times these buildings have been developed into flats and apartments.

(c. 1960) Furleys Wharf from the Riverside. This was one of the last working wharfs in Gainsborough (now demolished).

(c. 1910) Another view of the riverside warehouses looking towards the Trent Bridge. Today this area can be accessed by the Riverside walkway.

(c. 1980) Old Whittons Mill (now demolished), at the side of New Whittons Mill (now converted into flats). This building is easily recognised from the side, by its bright collage of colours.

(c. 1990) The old Baltic Mill (now demolished) and the back of the old Co-op (built 1907) today in use as a nightclub.

(c. 1990) Depicting Chapel Staithe which had steps providing access to the river in the days when Gainsborough was a busy river port. It was one of the most ancient areas of the old town. Once a meeting place, and where drinking water would be taken from river. The Delvers have recently placed a blue plaque on a lamppost on Chapel Staithe

(c. 1990) The old Rowing Club in the distance (now derelict), taken from the Nottinghamshire side of the Trent. The white box building, a product of 1960's, thinking, clearly stands out, but is soon to be redeveloped.

(c. 1960) Another view of the Old Chapel Staithe and adjacent buildings (now demolished) taken from the Riverside.

(c. 1960) The back of the Maltkins of Old Caskgate Street, which ran up to the Packet Landing (all now demolished). This area later became Whittons Gardens.

(c. 1960) The Packet Landing and the back of Red Hall (all now demolished) The council Guildhall building and car park was later built a short distance from this scene, which today forms part of Whittons Gardens.

(c. 1950) The Nottinghamshire side of the River Trent, on the path to the ship yard, in the vicinity of Dog Island. The old silo in the background (now demolished) has been replaced by a housing development.

(c. 1947) The 1947 floods at the allotments towards the rear of Fairway Avenue (today Queensfield).
St. Paul's Church Morton, is in the distance.

(c. 1950) A street party in Fairway Avenue (today Queensfield) St. Paul's Church, again in the distance.

(c. 1910) Morton Wharf depicting the Dutch influenced architecture. It was formerly the site of the Sailor Boy Inn. All of these buildings have now gone as the site is currently been developed for housing.

The Ægir, Gainsborough

(c. 1910) The Aegir at Morton Corner, with Morton Wharf in the distance. The Aegir, is Norse for, God of the Sea. A name lost in antiquity to describe the tidal bore of the River Trent.

Chapter Three: Bridge Street The ancient main thoroughfare, previously Le Southgate

(c. 1920) The Trent Bridge at Gainsborough, built in 1791 by Act of Parliament, seen with the old Toll Gates & the Toll Houses. It wasn't until May 1932 that the bridge was freed from tolls.

(c. 1960) Bridge Street as it appeared when turning left at the Trent Bridge, before the major 1960's demolition work had commenced. This area was once a busy and well populated area of the town with many people housed in yards, behind properties that fronted Bridge Street.

(c. 1960) The many pubs of Old Bridge Street were legendary. There were once in excess of 20 Pubs in this Gainsborough street alone – today none have survived. The Cross Keys Pub stood on Bridge Street adjacent to Thornton Street.

(c. 1920) Introducing Garnetts shop at 171 Bridge Street. The archway on the left led to Nottingham Place which was a yard housing a long row of small cottages. At the end of Nottingham Place were steps that led into King Street.

(c. 1960) The corner building was originally built for Captain Popplewell. His house featured a magnificent oval stairwell. Behind was a row of houses known as Popplewells Row. The building was later used as the old clinic and latterly became the corset factory (now demolished).

(c. 1960) The Stucco architecture of Captain Popplewell's can still be seen in the distance as we travel further up Bridge Street towards the town. The Bridge Inn Public House was located on the corner of Willoughby Street and Bridge Street.

(c. 1930) No finer house existed throughout the whole of the town than that of The Old Pillard House, Bridge Street. It stood opposite the Neptune Public House, and it is a crime that this building could not have been saved or preserved. It was rebuilt after the Civil War and had previously been a wealthy merchants residence.

(c. 1910) Another of the many pubs of Old Bridge Street. The Wheatsheaf Public House, was situated just past the Old Pillard House, and just beyond was The Queens Public House.

(c. 1960) The Ostrich Public House, boarded up and ready for demolition, stood in another very ancient area of the town, opposite Seven Foot Lane. The Delvers have recently placed a blue plaque, as part of their local history tours, in Seven Foot Lane

(c. 1945) A street party as part of the Victory in Europe celebrations held in Tooley Street, which is situated just off Bridge Street.

Chapter Four: Silver Street

The mercantile district that leads to the Market Place

(c. 1913) The Manchester Penny Bazaar of Silver Street later became Sills the furnishes, who had a retail presence in Gainsborough for most of the 20th century.

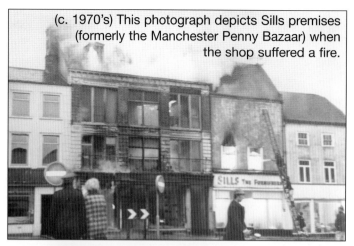

(c. 1970's) This photograph depicts Sills premises (formerly the Manchester Penny Bazaar) when the shop suffered a fire.

(c. 1989) Sills new store was relocated a short distance away, officially in Bridge Street (now demolished)
Wilkinson's hardware later moved to this site and established another new building.
Wilkinson's has now relocated to Marshall's Yard (Retail Park)

(c. 1912) Silver Street, looking towards the bridge, note Forrest & Hills Solicitors (Georgian) building on the right and the Baltic Mill (of Bridge St) in the distance.

(c. 1910) Showing Beales Photographers and Stevens Book & Records shop. The street was originally cobbled and called Silver St, as rents were payable in silver to the Lord of the Manor.

(c. 1910) As we look towards the Market Square, Bomers, Waterloo House is visible in the background, a reference to the halcyon days of Old Gainsborough.

(c. 1951) A busy scene on Silver Street, looking towards the Market Square. Jays furniture store is visible on the right, as are the blinds on Bomer & Co. These were ritually displayed first thing in the morning to protect merchandise from the sunlight.

(c. 1989) This ariel view shows the Market Square prior to being pedestrianised and the landscaping which was part of a development of the 1990's.

(c. 1989) The Co-op before the Lindsey Centre development commenced. Overleaf the same scene 70 years earlier.

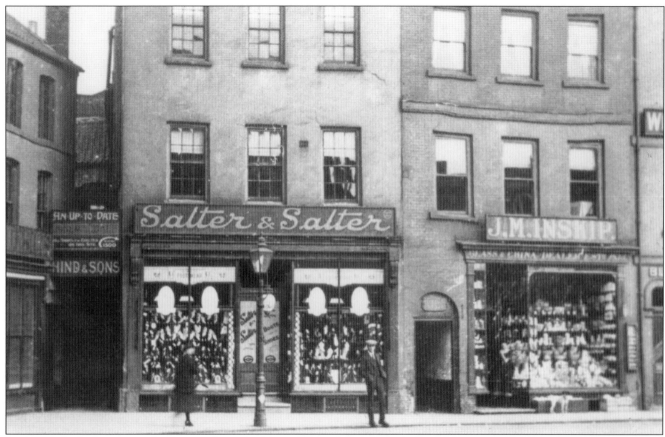

(c. 1920) A similar scene to the previous, but in a different time. Hinds Bread Shop, Salter & Salter Boot Co, and Inskips China Shop (all now demolished). The Grand and Geaumont cinemas also are remembered as history connected to this site. The entire site was eventually acquired by the Lincoln Co-operative Society.

THE MARKET PLACE, GAINSBOROUGH

(c. 1910) The Market Square, complete with cobble stones and the (new) Town Hall at the centre of the picture. This building was badly affected by bombs dropped nearby in 1942. The bombs missed their intended target – Marshalls engineering works.

(c. 1955) Busy market day scene with the (mock) Georgian styled Provisional Bank (today Nat West) having survived. This photograph was taken before the widening of Church Street.
The diagonal black and white building was known as Belton's Pen Corner.

Chapter Five: Church Street

The historic district at the heart of the town

(c. 1960) The demolition of Belton's Pen Corner, to enable the widening of Church Street and Market Street.

(c. 1920) A scene in Church Street at the bottom of Roseway before it was knocked through for traffic (1932), The Horse & Jockey Public House is situated on the right.

(c. 1960) A photograph of the Church Street shops at the corner of Gladstone Street, seen here boarded up, prior to demolition and street widening 1962.

(c. 1960) Church Street seen here before the demolition of the small shops on the right, which all disappeared as far as The Friendship Inn, which currently is being converted into flats.

(c. 1950) The All Saints Parish Church, complete with grave stones (now gone) was once the only Church of the town. This photograph was taken before the Church grounds were landscaped.

(c. 1998) The Parish Church, depicting the countdown to the millennium.

(c. 1910) The Old Plough Inn on Church Street.

(c. 1918) The Parish Church School depicting a physical training lesson. Thornton Square built 1777 is in background (only recently demolished).

(c. 2003) Back of Thornton Square, Church Street (now demolished). The lessons of the past do not appear to have been learned. This entire area (opposite Acland Street) has recently been demolished and has hurriedly been built on. Further developments are planned and The Delvers hope to place a further blue plaque shortly to mark the history connected to this historical area.

Chapter Six: Ashcroft Road/Trinity Street The Victorian new town – which expanded onto The Prairie

(c. 1990) Vigilans. Meaning to be alert. The 1887 plaque on the building, is in the Parish of St. Johns.

(c. 1930) Vigilans, the intended living quarters to house a college of Priests, originally built under the patronage of Sir Hickman Bacon. (today used as flats)

(c. 1960) St Johns Bridge, Strafford Street, looking down from Sandsfield Lane, once the site of a Rope Walk. It is interesting to note most of the streets on the Prairie (Sandsfield Lane) had a corner shop during most of the 20th century.

(c. 1960) Bridge Road, at the top of King Street, showing a row of houses on the right (now demolished) replaced by Style Homes. The corner building is currently the site of the Fishing Tackle shop.

(c. 1960) This photograph shows the splendid Adelaide Terrace, on the corner of Bridge Road. Down a side passage was Adelaide Gardens. Note the roundabout which subsequently was demolished only to be resurrected in the 21st century at what is today Thorndike Way. History repeats itself.

(c. 1960) Hoopers Grocery shop at the bottom of Marlborough Street, which was demolished along with one side of Wellington Street to make way for the "New Road", Thorndike Way.

(c. 1980) The Yarborough junction after the building of the New Road.

(c. 1910) Ashcroft House which was built as a boys boarding and day school by Mr Robinson a Unitarian Minister, later to become the Yarborough Hotel.

Trinity Street, Gainsborough.

(c. 1920) Trinity Street looking towards the town. Parkinsons Newsagents on the left had a shop for many years in this area.

(c. 1960) This photograph depicts the Beer Off License at the top of Willoughby Street complete with beer barrels outside the shop (today Caddy's Kabin).

(c. 1960) Inside the Holy Trinity Church. After this church closed the building commenced a new life as the Trinity Arts Centre and cinema.

(c. 1960) This photograph shows Pillard House Lane to the right and Trinity Church steeple in the background. The Gainsborough fair took place on this site in the 1950's.

(c. 1950) The underground toilets at Southolme (now demolished). Today the busy Tesco junction.

(c. 1999) The demolition of Marshalls (paint shop), on the Southolme, which later became the site of Tesco's supermarket. Marshalls agricultural engineering works once dominated Gainsborough. During the first World War Marshalls works employed over 5000 men & women and exported worldwide.

(c. 1910) This photograph shows the crowds of workmen leaving Marshalls or "The Works" for their lunch.
The buzzer would sound once at 12 noon to inform the workers that their lunch hour had commenced and sound a second time at 12.50 - a timely reminder for the men to get back to work! A third and final buzzer would sound at 1.00pm.

(c. 1960) A fragment of old Gainsborough. This photograph shows Station Hill which led to the once magnificent Great Central Railway Station. Pingle Hill is on the right, Marshalls Works are on the left, which today is an entrance to the site of Marshalls Yard Retail Park.

(c. 1910) Until the 1960's the Great Central Railway Station was a very busy railway junction especially for coastal journeys, where excited children look forward to a day at the seaside. The station was well equipped and is remembered for its comfortable ladies waiting room with a real coal fire in the winter months.

Chapter Seven: North Street Running parallel to Church Street

(c. 1960) This photograph was taken at the time of the road widening looking down Roseway from North Street. The Horse & Jockey public house (the white building) clearly stands out on the corner.

(c. 1960) North Street, from the top of New Street, perhaps the smallest street in Gainsborough? Clearly visible are the tall chimneys of Alma Place with the gas works in the background.

(c. 1962) This delightful photograph shows a queue forming for a football match on the Northolme, before the Blues Club was built. There was always a policeman present to keep the crowds in order. Entrance was gained by the large gates or by the turnstiles.

(c. 1910) An older view of the Elm Cottage public house, complete with the very narrow road which led to Back Street (later North Street), as Church Street was the main thoroughfare at this time.

(c. 1960) A later view of the Elm Cottage public house with the gas works on the right, looking down Church Street and Gas Works cottages.

(c. 1989) Looking into Spring Gardens, Cassie Watts Antiques shop was there for many years.
These buildings and The Horse & Groom public house were of Dutch influenced architecture built around 1910 (all now demolished). Cassie Watts has now been rebuilt as apartments in a similar style. The former Horse & Groom is now situated around the main entrance to Marshalls Yard Retail Park.

(c. 1989) Showing Market Street looking towards Lord Street. The Peacock Public House was on the site of todays Lloyds TSB Bank and on the opposite side of the street was The Marquis of Granby. Both public houses were destroyed when Market Street was hit by bombs in 1942.

(c. 1950) Depicting Market Street looking towards the old County Court. The town buses stopped outside Currys for Lea. The bus stop for Morton was outside Meeds Wine shop. The bus in the picture is situated where The Marquis of Granby public house once stood.

Market Hall, Gainsborough

(c. 1920) Lord Street showing the Peacock Hotel, the tall building on the far right hand side of the road. The New Town Hall (now The Sands venue) was built in 1908. The corner shop was Dixons Drapery but is now Halifax plc.

(c. 1990) Showing the sign of Amcotes Book Sellers, Printers & Stationers (Later acquired by Beltons). The ornate tiled entrance to Beecheys, who also once operated from these premises, can still be seen today.

(c. 1910) This picture of Lord Street, shows Stovins shop on the left with two people standing outside. Mr Stovin was a pork butcher. He always opened the windows very wide and had sawdust on the floor. The left hand side of Lord Street is very much the same today, the White Hart Hotel is in the distance.

(c. 1900) The White Lion public house. The archway on the right was to White Lion Yard, which one time provided stabling. It finished as a public house in 1913.

(c. 1915) A delightful photograph of Nellie Housham taken around the time of the Great War. The site was demolished and later became the Gainsborough Building Society during the 1960's.

(c. 1910) The old Woolpack public house, Caskgate Street stood to the left. People would stay overnight at the Woolpack and catch the steam packet up to Hull, which departed from nearby Packet Landing.

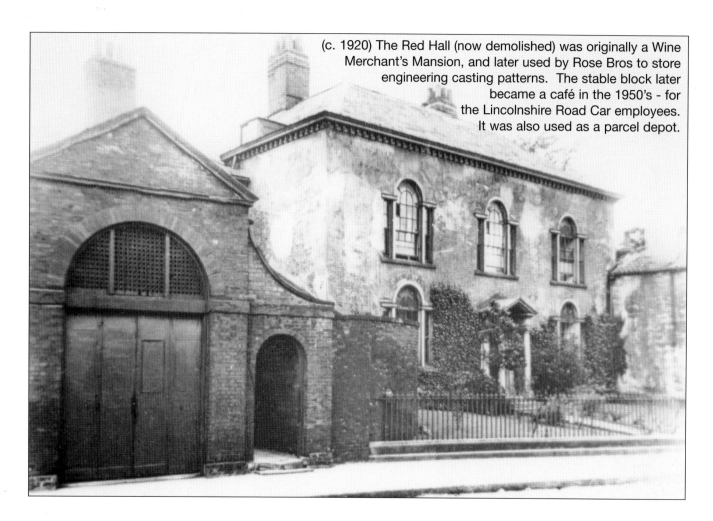

(c. 1920) The Red Hall (now demolished) was originally a Wine Merchant's Mansion, and later used by Rose Bros to store engineering casting patterns. The stable block later became a café in the 1950's - for the Lincolnshire Road Car employees. It was also used as a parcel depot.

(c. 1910) Gainsborough Trent Bridge showing the old towpath underneath.
An 18th century gateway to a 21st century town?